101 FOOD JOKES

THE HENNESSY KIDS

101 Food Jokes / by The Hennessy Kids

ISBN 978-1-989621-04-2 (Print)

ISBN 978-1-989621-05-9 (E-book)

1. Wit and humor, Juvenile. 2. English wit and humor. I. The Hennessy Kids, author

The Hennessy Kids | TheHennessyKids.com | instagram.com/thehennessykids twitter.com/thehennessykids

First Printing, 2020

For all of our taste buds.

FOOD JOKES

What has T in the beginning, T in the middle, and T at the end?
   A teapot.

A fast food employee dropped my burger patty on the floor before serving it to me. They said it was ground beef.

Dan: Why don't you wanna taco 'bout it?
   Sam: Because I'm nacho friend anymore.

Sam: There is a fly in my soup.
   Katherine: Don't worry, the spider in your bread will get it.

Dad, will my pizza be long?
   No, it will be round.

. . .

Did you hear about the fast food at the monastery?
    There's a chip monk and a fish friar.

Did you hear about the new restaurant in outer space?
    The food is great but there's no atmosphere.

Did you hear the joke about the peanut butter?
    I'm not telling you. You might spread it.

Did you see the movie about the hot dog?
    It was an Oscar Wiener.

Every morning I think I'm going to make pancakes, but I keep
waffling.

Have you heard the joke about the pizza?
    Never mind, it's too cheesy.

How do you get fat free milk?
    From a skinny cow.

What's the easiest way to find an elephant?
    Hide in a bush and make a noise like a peanut.

How do you know carrots are good for your eyes?
    Have you ever seen a rabbit wearing glasses?.

. . .

How do you make a milk shake?
    Give it a good scare.

How do you make a sausage roll?
    Push it down the hill.

How do you make a walnut laugh?
    Crack it up.

How do you make an apple turnover?
    Push it down the hill, too.

How fast is milk?
    It's pasteurized before you know it.

Where do you learn to make ice cream?
    Sundae school.

My dad hurt himself eating seafood.
    He pulled a mussel.

My friend won't take to me any more because of my obsession
with pasta.
    I'm feeling cannelloni right now.

. . .

My teacher bet me a hundred dollars I couldn't build a plane out of spaghetti.
  You should have seen the look on her face as I flew pasta.

Waiter, this food tastes kind of funny.
  Then why aren't you laughing?

What are twins' favourite fruit?
  Pears.

What can you put in a freezer that's hot but will always come out hot?
  Hot sauce.

What candy do you eat during school break?
  Recess pieces.

What cheese is made backwards?
  Edam.

What cheese is not yours?
  Nacho cheese.

What did Bacon say to Tomato?
  Lettuce get out of here.

. . .

What did one blueberry say to the other blueberry?
If you weren't so sweet, we wouldn't be in this jam.

What did the baby corn say to the mama corn?
"Where's pop corn?"

What did the banana say to its sick friend?
How are you peeling?

What did the bragging pickle say?
I'm kind of a big dill.

What did the cupcake say to the icing?
I'd be muffin without you.

What did the frog order at McDonald's?
French flies and a diet croak.

What did the frozen treat's friend say when it turned ten years old?
It's sherbert day.

What did the ghost put on his bagel?
Scream cheese.

What did the gingerbread man find on his bed?

A cookie sheet.

What did the happy slice of cheese say to the sad slice of cheese?
"It will turn out okay. Everything is gouda."

What did the hot dog say when his friend passed him in the race?
Wow, I relish the fact that you've mustard the strength to ketchup to me.

What did the hot dog bun say to the sourdough?
You're my roll model.

What did the pecan say to the walnut?
We're friends because we're both nuts.

What did the snowman order at the restaurant?
An iceberger with chili sauce.

Are you a vegetable, animal, or mineral?
Vegetable - I'm a human bean.

What did the tomato say to the other tomato?
"You go on without me, I'll ketchup."

What did the waiter say when he dropped a hotdog?
It could always be wurst.

. . .

What do elves make sandwiches with?
    Shortbread

What do ghosts serve for dessert?
    Ice scream and booberries.

What do race car driver's eat?
    Fast food.

What do snowmen eat for breakfast?
    Frosted Flakes or Ice Crispies.

My brother told me an onion is the only food that makes you cry.
    So I dropped a pineapple on his foot.

What did the student say after the teacher said, "Order, students, order?"
    "Can I have fries and a burger?"

Two cookies are baking in an oven. One cookie says to the other, "Man, is it me, or is it getting kinda hot in here?"
    The other cookie replies, "Oh my goodness. A talking cookie."

EVEN MORE FOOD JOKES

What is worse than finding half a worm in your apple?
    Spitting the other half out.

Why did the boy throw butter out the window?
    To see butter fly.

What do you call a cashew at the space station?
    An astronut.

What do you call a fake noodle?
    An impasta.

What do you call a mac 'n' cheese that gets all up in your face?
    Too close for comfort food.

. . .

What do you call a sheep covered in chocolate?
     I don't know, a Hershey baah?

What do you call a train full of bubble gum?
     A chew-chew train.

What do you call an avocado that's been blessed?
     Holy guacamole.

What do you call cheese that isn't yours?
     Nacho cheese.

What do you call the time in between eating peaches?
     A pit-stop.

What do you call three raspberries playing music?
     A jam session.

What do you call two bananas?
     A pair of slippers.

What do you get when a pig and a chicken bump into each other?
     Ham and eggs.

What do you get when you cross a hot dog and Halloween?

A Hallo-weenie.

What do you give to a sick lemon?
    Lemon aid.

What did the psychic order at McDonald's?
    Medium fries.

What do you say to a sad salad?
    Don't kale my vibe.

What does a nosey pepper do?
    Get jalapeño business.

What does an orange do when it takes a juice test?
    It concentrates.

What does it do before it rains cupcakes?
    It sprinkles.

What fruit do you need if you're locked out?
    A key-wi.

What happened when the strawberry was run over?
    It created a traffic jam.

. . .

What happens when veggies throw a party?
　　They get a DJ to turnip the beet.

What has to be broken before you can use it?
　　An egg.

What is a math teacher's favourite dessert?
　　Pi.

What is a pretzel's favourite dance?
　　The twist.

What is a table you can eat?
　　A vegetable.

What is a taxi driver's favourite kind of vegetable?
　　A cab-bage

What is a witch's favourite food?
　　Ghoulash.

What is Beethoven's favourite fruit?
　　Ban-ana-na.

What is black; white, green and bumpy?
　　A pickle wearing a tuxedo.

. . .

What is green and sings?
    Elvis Parsley

What is green and white when it is up and red when it hits the ground?
    A watermelon.

What is green, small and round and goes up and down?
    A pea in an elevator.

What is small, red and has a sore throat?
    A hoarse radish.

What is the most attractive fruit?
    A fine-apple.

What is white, has a horn, and gives milk?
    A dairy truck.

What kind of keys do kids like to carry?
    Cookies.

What kind of nut always seems to have a cold?
    Cashew.

. . .

What do you get when you mix a dog with a daisy?
    A collie-flower.

What kind of vegetable likes to look at animals?
    A zoo-chini.

What kind of vegetable truck need when it had a flat tire?
    A-spare-agus.

What type of candy is never on time?
    Choco-late.

What type of vegetable looks after the elderly?
    The carrot-aker.

What vegetable has eyes but can't see?
    A potato.

What vegetables can't you take on a boat?
    Leeks.

What's an apple's favourite compliment?
    You're awesome to the core.

What's Peter Pan's favourite fast food restaurant?
    Wendy's.

. . .

What's Santa's favourite candy?
  Jolly Ranchers.

What's the best thing to put into a pie?
  Your teeth.

What's the most emotional food at her wedding?
  The wedding cake - it's always in tiers.

What's white on the inside and green on the outside?
  A banana dressed up as a cucumber.

What's white, red and blue at Christmas time?
  A sad candy cane.

What's a baker's favourite joke?
  A cinnamon pun.

What's a ghost's favourite desert?
  Boo-berry ice scream.

What's a penguin's favourite salad ingredient?
  Iceberg lettuce

YET MORE FOOD JOKES

What's a potato Jedi's worst enemy?
  Darth Tater.

What's a tailor's favourite kind of vegetable?
  A string bean.

What's a vegetable's favourite martial art?
  Carr-o-tee.

What's an egg's least favourite day of the week?
  Fry-day.

What's better than a good friend?
  A good friend with chocolate.

. . .

What's orange and sounds like a parrot?
    A carrot.

What's the sound kids make who love their vegetables?
    Brussel shouts.

When do astronauts eat?
    At launch time.

When potatoes have babies, what are they called?
    Tater tots.

When should you take a cookie to the doctor?
    When it feels crummy.

Whenever I want to start eating healthy a chocolate bar looks at me and snickers.

Where did the spaghetti go to dance?
    The meat ball.

Where do ghosts buy their food?
    At the ghostery store.

Where does the Easter bunny eat breakfast?
    IHOP.

. . .

Why can't eggs tell jokes?
    They'd crack each other up.

Why can't you trust overloaded tacos?
    Because they spill the beans.

Why couldn't the sesame seed leave the gambling casino
    Because he was on a roll.

Why did that kid just swallow the money his mom gave you?
    He was told it was lunch money.

Why did the bacon laugh?
    Because the egg cracked a yoke.

Why did the baker stop making doughnuts?
    He was annoyed with the hole business.

Why did the banana go out with the prune?
    Because he couldn't find a date.

Why did the banana go to the doctor?
    Because it wasn't peeling well.

. . .

Why did the butcher work overtime last week?
    To make ends meat.

Why did the chef have to stop cooking with herbs?
    He ran out of thyme.

Why did the chicken join the band?
    Because he had the drumsticks.

Why did the cookie cry?
    Because his mother was a wafer too long.

Why did the cow eat the tight rope walker?
    Because he wanted a balanced meal.

Why was the egg sad it was in an omelet?
    It wasn't all it cracked up to be.

Why did the fisherman put peanut butter into the sea?
    To go with the jellyfish.

Why did the gardener quit?
    Because his celery wasn't high enough.

Why did the hamburger go to the gym?
    It wanted better buns.

. . .

Why did the ice-cream truck break down?
  Because of the rocky road.

Why did the jellybean go to school?
  To become a smartie.

Why did the lady love to drink hot chocolate?
  Because she was a cocoanut.

Why did the skeleton go to the barbecue?
  To get a spare rib.

Why did the students eat their homework?
  Because the teacher said that it was a piece of cake.

Why did the tofu cross the road?
  To prove it wasn't chicken.

Why do melons have fancy weddings?
  Because they cantaloupe.

Why do the French eat snails?
  Because they don't like fast food.

. . .

Why do they only eat one egg for breakfast in France?
    Because in France, one egg is an oeuf.

Why does the mushroom always get invited to parties?
    Because he's a fun-gi.

Why does yogurt love going to the museum?
    Because it's cultured.

Why does your dad keep candy canes locked away?
    He keeps them in mint condition.

Why doesn't anyone laugh at the gardener's jokes?
    Because they're too corny.

Why don't they serve chocolate in prison?
    Because it makes you break out.

Why shouldn't you tell a secret on a farm?
    Because the potatoes have eyes and the corn has ears.

Why was the bread dough sad?
    It wanted to be kneaded by someone.

WORD SEARCH

```
G Y E Y S P X F X Y H N K G P
L R F L U A N L R L Q R D E O
U Z A O F J N R J T C O A B K
G H S P P F E D N R O C P O P
A U O H E B A C W A H P T E M
Z N M T P Y U W E I M I O L U
E C A S D P A N L L C E R P F
P T A N C O A M P M Y H R P F
A R A A A C G A P I Q L A A I
S C K L H B S U A X H E C W N
T E Q O O E S R E Q Y S E G U
A I S D K C D O N U T H U Q E
F A J I T A O T I I S U D S N
E E G N A R O H P A Z Z I P U
T A C O Q U K I C E C R E A M
```

APPLE	GRAPE	PINEAPPLE
BANANA	GUM	PIZZA
CANDY	HOTDOG	POPCORN
CARROT	ICE CREAM	RASPBERRY
CASHEW	MUFFIN	SANDWICH
CHOCOLATE	NACHOS	SOUP
CORN	ORANGE	SUSHI
CUPCAKE	PASTA	TACO
DONUT	PEACH	TRAIL MIX
FAJITA	PIE	WAFFLE

ONE OF OUR RECIPES

A quick & easy recipe for rice crispy squares!

5 cups marshmallows (about 40 regular
large marshmallows)
1/4 cup butter
1 teaspoon vanilla
5 cups rice crisp cereal

- Using a soup pot, melt marshmallows and butter over medium-low heat. Make sure to stir it constantly for a few minutes until it is all smooth.
- Take the soup pot off the heat and then stir in the teaspoon of vanilla.
- Next, you add 2-1/2 cups of rice crisp cereal and stir until coated in stickiness.

- Then pour in the second half of the nice crisp cereal and mix it up so it is all coated, too.
- Use butter or margarine to grease an 11" by 7" glass baking dish or metal cake pan, then scrape the mix from the pot into the dish and level it out.
- Let it cool down, and when it is cooled down then cut it into squares.
- Share it with your taste buds!

COMING SOON

We are working on a recipe book!

YOUR FAVOURITE JOKE

What is your favourite food joke that isn't in this book?

Visit www.thehennessykids.com and submit your own joke,
or email us at thehennessykids@gmail.com!

Thank you for reading our book! We hope you enjoyed it.

We think the world would be better with more smiles. Please tell these jokes to your friends and family and make more people happy.

ABOUT THE AUTHORS

This is The Hennessy Kids' sixth joke book. For more fun stuff, find them online as @TheHennessyKids on Twitter, Instagram, and Facebook, and visit them on thehennessykids.com!

ALSO BY THE HENNESSY KIDS

Visit thehennessykids.com and join our reader's list to be the first to find out when our books are coming out!

CPSIA information can be obtained
at www.ICGtesting.com
Printed in the USA
BVHW040721190821
614614BV00018B/1318

9 781989 621042